Genealogy 101
Starting your Family Tree
By Catherine Coulter

Other workbooks in The Family Tree Research Workbook series

Written By Catherine Coulter

Land Research Records

Census Research Record

My Family Research Plan

Military Research Records

Web Log and Web Accounts

Immigration Research Records

Court House Research Records

Family Group Research Record

Naturalization Research Records

My Family Tree Research Record

My Family Tree Research Notebook

Cemetery and Funeral Home Research Records

Let this workbook series help you while Following the Path of Your Ancestors.

Hello, I would like to welcome to Genealogy 101. Tonight some of the things I will be talking about are how to start your family tree **creating a research plan and mistakes that can be made**

I am sure many of you have asked your selves, how do I start? Well the answer is that **you begin with yourself** and with what you already know and work from there.

It sounds simple and you may wonder why when what you want to know may be two generations or more back. The information you gather on each generation as you go backward will give you clues on where to look for information on the next generation.

It is very much like a puzzle with the pieces scattered on the floor. You never know for sure which piece you will find next and how it will lead to the next puzzle piece being found. But in the end you will have a nice picture of your family tree.

For example, let's say you know your grandmothers birth date and the place of her birth, but not her parents. Your Grandmother's birth information will aid you in finding the records for her and that will give you the parents' names and a bit of information leading you backward in the family tree.

Having your grandmother's brothers and sisters names and their birth information will help insure you are finding the right records.

Once you have gathered all that you know it's time to look at the family documents and records to verify your information and to help look for any information you do not already have.

There are many kinds of family documents and records that can be beneficial to a genealogist. Birth, death, and marriage records are the basic ones that everyone thinks of right away.

But there are more that can be quite helpful. Family Bibles, Photo Albums, Scrapbooks, and Diaries can have Birth, Marriage, Death records in them, and possibly divorce information.

Sometimes you may find newspaper articles, obituaries, letters, or notes tucked inside. Some other documents and records are Military records, Letters, Baby Books, and any family trees someone else in the family may have already done. Keep in mind that if you do not have some of these types of documents and records for your ancestors a family member might.

Contacting your relatives to see if they can help you fill in gaps, show you family documents and records they have or even tell you stories about your family is the next step.

If they have documents or records that they are willing to share with you be sure to ask if they will photo copy them for you. If not take down as much information from them as you can the first time you view them. Be sure you ask if you can take a photo of them too.

Knowing what questions you want to ask and the information you are looking for will give you the best results but you need to be specific about the people, events, or dates you are asking about.

 For example, instead of asking what do you know about your grandfather? You ask instead, what was your grandfather's job or how old was your grandmother when she got married.

Having the questions ready and written down will keep you focused and so you will not forget anything important you wanted to ask. Once you have asked a question that's on your list don't forget to check it off as you continue on.

You will also want to make notes about other questions that may arise during the conversation. Above all write down everything you can or record the conversation.

Keep in mind though you will need to verify any information you receive other than the documents you have been shown.

When you have all of the information on yourself and other relatives that you were able to gather, it is time to get serious about getting organized. It is likely most the important thing you can do when starting your family tree.

Being organized will enable you to do your research without stopping to search for information you know you have and what it is you need. Also having your research organized will insure that you don't lose information or find it lost amongst other surnames you want to research.

The first step in getting organized is to create a research plan. Your research plan will be very important to you and you will find yourself referring to it often. Creating a research plan that will aid you greatly in your research can be very easy to make.

You will want a check list of documents and records for family members you have talked to You may want to add beside the name of the family member you talked to whether or not they were able to help you.

It would be good idea to ask anyone you do talk to get in touch with you if they think of anything that may help you. Who knows they just might be able to after a bit.

You will be visiting or contacting many different places and people as you do your research. Having a contact list is also important. Do not just keep the phone number but also get the address and the person's name you talked to.

You will want to keep track of the hours of operation and what resources they have. You never know when you will need this information later on. This list can be a big help as well in keeping you from contacting someone about a particular ancestor that you already.

This Contact list should also include the relatives you have talked to and which ancestors you talked about. Try to refer this information to the notes that you took or the recording you made of the conversation and any copies of documents that you were able to obtain.

It helps keep you from going back and trying to gather information you already have. If a question would come up or you need a bit more clarification on the information this would let you know who you need to contact again to do so.

Keeping a list of internet sites you have used or wish to use is valuable as well as long as you can keep track of the many data bases you have used or plan to use at each site.

Don't forget to make a notation of any database you have searched for each website so you will not have to find out you already looked there. Having a *Web Log and Web Accounts* book would be helpful to do this.

Making a list of books you have want to look at or have searched for information on your ancestors. If you have found information in a book make a note of which book the author and page you found the information. That way if you need to go back to look at it again you will have all you need to find the information again easily. I have published a book that may help you do just that it is called *My Family Tree Research Plan.* It is designed to aid you in planning your research needs and guide you in your research.

The next step in your Organizing is to create and maintain a filing system that will be easy to use. You need to be able to create a way of filing your documents, records, and information you will be gathering. There are many ways to do this and don't be surprised if you find yourself using more than one or changing the way you do this over time.

One way is to use a three ring binder. With a three ring binder you have a good way to organize each family surname you are working with. By placing one surname in one binder you would keep the family members all in one place using dividers to separate individuals.

Documents and photocopies could be stored in a division of their own such as marriage in one and birth in another or put them with each ancestor they are associated with.

Don't forget to use top loading sheet protectors to hold papers and documents that you do not want to put holes into but want to be able to view them. Sheet protectors are a great asset to use with a three ring binder.

File folders can be used but I advise that if you use file folders you have a filing cabinet or file boxes to hold them as well as using something to hold the papers into the folder. I have used rubber bands, paper clamps, paper clips (they tend to fall off though), or staple them.

Each file folder depending on how you use them can contain information on several family members or just one individual.

I have use them both ways and prefer each individual have their own file folder to hold documents for them and notes or research I have not yet added to my computer program or binder. I tend to use a file folder as a temporary file for my research.

As for computer programs, there are many different programs that will help you with your family tree. Each one has their good points and bad points.

If you chose to use a computer program make sure it will be easy for you to use and can produce genealogy reports and charts. Read reviews on them to see what others like and don't like about them.

Read both good and the bad reviews because each will tell you more that if that person liked or hated the program. While reading these reviews, keep in mind there are some companies that may post their own reviews or post on competitors sites as well.

Also make sure it will work with your operating system of your own computer. I cannot say what program to use because it is a personal choice and what I use or would use may not work for you.

I can advise though that if you are keeping information for your family tree on a computer to keep a backup copy of all of the information. Use either a flash drive or cd or even paper form or all three. But keep a backup just the same. Computers have been known to fail and lose information. You would not want to do all of this work only to lose everything if your computer crashes.

It is a good idea to have various blank forms on hand that you will be using when researching. The various forms you will need are Family Group Sheets, Census Logs, Cemetery Forms and Ancestor Charts to name a few.

Family Group Sheets will help you organize your information and prepare it to be entered into a computer program, book, or chart. It will also show you what information is missing and what you have.

A family group sheet is a great research tool to take with you on research trips to the library, historical societies, and anywhere your research takes you.

The Family Group Sheets usually include the usual information such as name of ancestor, dates, and notes for the following information: birth, death, buried, parents, marriages, spouses, and children with their birth and death dates, also places they were born.

The next two pages are an example of a Family Group Sheet I created. It holds places for more information than you can find on other group sheets and is easier to use. It gives you the flexibility to add your own categories of information to the sheet that you may find. I have published a Book called *Family Group Research Records* that has usable Family Group Sheets for your convince, checklists, and information to help you with your research.

Example: Page 1 of the Family Group Sheet

Family Group Sheet

Ancestor's Name_____James Luthar Griffin_____

Event	Month	Day	Year	Notes	Notes #
Born	March	18	1839	Butler Co. Pa	
Died	April	25	1923	Hendersonville Worth Twp	1
Buried				Irwin Cemetery Irwin Twp.	2
Father B			1804	James Griffin	
D					
Mother B			1799	Elizabeth Kohlmeyer	
D			1856		
Married 1	August	17	1862		
Spouse 1 B	October	20	1876	Flora Kerr	
D	Jan	20	1935	Sandy Lake Mercer Co. pa	3
Spouse 2 B					
D					
Occupation				Carpenter Learned this in Ill.	
Residence			1856	Livingston Co. Illinois	
Residence			1880	Mercer County Pennsylvania	
Military				Civil War 140th Pennsylvania	

Children:

	Name	Birth	Place of Birth	Death	#
1. M	Orville Folett	May 16, 1867	Mercer Co. Pa	1942	
2. F	Magie	1886			
3. F	Mable	Dec 7, 1871			
4.					
5.					
6.					
7.					

Example: Page 2 of the Family Group Sheet

Children:

	Name	Birth	Place of Birth	Death	#
8.					
9					
10					
10					
11					
12					

U.S. Federal Census

	State	County	Township	Notes	#
1790					
1800					
1810					
1820					
1830					
1840					
1850					
1860	Illinois	Livingston	Reading		
1870					
1880	Pennsylvania	Mercer	Worth		
1890					
1900					
1910	Pennsylvania	Mercer	Worth		
1920					
1930					
1940					

Notes:

1) Mercer County Pa. In his home.
2) Venango County Pa 10 miles east of Mercer County Pa boarder
3) In her home near Sandy Lake – Grove City Mercer County Pa

Census logs will be a huge help in keeping track of the many census records you will be viewing. They will help you keep track of the census records you have found of each individual in a surname.

The log would give you their name, state, county, and township they lived in for that census year but also the book number page number and the line number of the census record you found. This information will let you go back to view the record again and it will help you cite the information if you wish to share your families information with others.

The next page is an example of my Census logs that can be found in the book *Census Research Records*. In this book as well it explains the kinds of information that you can find on the different census records that are available for you to research as well as other important information that will help you with these records.

Example: Census Log

Census Log

Census Year _____1900_____   Page # __1__

#	Name	State	County	Township	Book #	Page #	Line#
1.	Henry J.	Pa	Schuylkill	Shenandoah		246	8
2.	Gertrude	Pa	Schuylkill	Shenandoah		246	8
3.							
4.							
5.							
6.							
7.							
8.							
9.							
10.							
11.							

Cemetery Record Forms are very helpful when trying to locate the grave sites of your ancestors or to record the information on ones you already know. It will give you not only the cemetery name, its location, and contact information but can have a place for a web site hours of operation for the office and a place to write down the directions to the cemetery.

Then it should have a place for you to record the information about the ancestor you are looking for. This information should include the date of burial section number and lot number to make finding them easier.

The form should also have a spot to add the funeral home that was used and its contact information and a place for listing other family members who are buried nearby as well.

Funeral Home Records can provide you with little known information. The funeral As with the cemetery records these forms will give you contact information, hours and directions to get there as well as your ancestors information and cemetery they were buried in.

The next page is an example of the Cemetery Record Forms and the Funeral Home Records that you can find in the *Cemetery and Funeral home Research Records* I have published. This book has information to help you researching these records as well.

Example: Cemetery Research Record

Cemetery Research Record

Cemetery Name___Oak Hill __
Location___Sandy Lake Mercer Co. Pennsylvania
Address__Rt Pa 173_& Cemetery Road_____
Phone Number___(724) 376-3558__
Email_____
Website_____
Person Contacted_____

Method of Contact used   Hours   Directions
   Ancestor looking for; (additional Ancestors for this cemetery on back)
   Name_John Lean
   Birth/Death Dates_____1853 - 1919
   Confirmation of Burial Y / N   Date of Burial_____   **Section**
   Number _____**Lot #**_____
      Copies of: **Death Certificate**_____ **Obituary**____ **Burial Record**____
      Family Members associated with the
   lot_____

Funeral Home
used_____
      Address_____
      Phone Number_____
      Email_____
Other Family members found buried nearby (Don't forget to add their dates)
_____
_____
_____

Example: Funeral Home Forms

Funeral Home Form

Funeral Home Name__Cunningham Funeral Home_ Notes:_____

Location___Grove City Mercer County Pa.__ _____

Address 306 Bessemer Avenue, Grove City, PA 16127 _____

Phone Number_(724) 458-7790

Email__cngm@verizon.net<cngm@verizon.net_

Website__http://www.cunninghamfhgc.com/fh/home/home.cfm?fh_id=12841

Method of contact used: Hours: Directions:

Ancestor looking for: (additional Ancestors for this cemetery on back**)**

Name_ Rachael Coulter ____ **Birth/Death Dates**__1862 - 1938

Confirmation of Funeral Y / N Date of Funeral_____

Date of Burial_____

 Copies of: Death Certificate_____ Obituary____ Burial Record____

Family Members associated with the Funeral Home_____

_____

Cemetery used__Woodland Cemetery_____

 Address_____ 211 South Center St Grove City Pa_____

 PhoneNumber____ (724) 458-6640_____

 Email_____

Notes_ Plot section 1 lot 418w grave 2_____

_____

An ancestor chart is like a road map of a family. It will map out the relationships and depending on the one you use it will give a space for some information as well. Usually the information is most often only the main dates associated with each individual such as year of birth and death (1850-1899). Some do though offer more information.

The number of generations they can have is also varying. They can be as few as 3-5 generations or as many as 20. The shape of the ancestor charts and how they are formatted are also varying.

It usually depends on how you want it to look and what you want it to say about your family. A very common and well known Ancestor/ Descendant Chart is that of the Family TREE Chart.

There are other forms that can be used to map out your family. The more typical ones are that of a Pedigree Chart, Descendant Chart, Hourglass Chart, and Fan Charts. There are also Vertical Pedigree Charts, Horizontal Hourglass Charts, and Bow Tie Charts as well.

The ancestor/ descendant charts can be very simple and plain or be quite elaborate and decorative. In any case they are useful in helping to map out relationships and to be used as a quick reference to the family dynamic as well as vital dates if they have them. They are well worth the time and effort to fill them out.

Once you have gathered all of the information you and your family know and are organized you are ready to begin researching your family tree. You will need to fill in any gaps that you have in your information that you have. The first thing needed now is deciding which branch of your tree you will start with.

Once you have that decision made you can start to fill out a family group sheet and plan a more detailed search for that ancestor. Planning will save you time and enable you to schedule visits to Court Houses, Historical Societies, and other places you may need to go.

Two of the documents you will want to search are Cemetery Records and Census Records. Researching cemetery records can usually be done online or through a Historical Society and through Libraries. Two free online sites I have found useful is *Find a Grave.com* and *Interment.*

Sometimes you will find a county cemetery indexes like we have here at the Historical Society which makes it easier to find your ancestors in the cemetery books we have. You can of course contact different cemeteries near where your ancestors lived as well as funeral homes in the area where they died.

You could visit the cemeteries and search that way as well. Contacting the cemeteries is something I would suggest you do to see what information you can gather from them on your ancestors.

When you go to the cemetery and find the head stone you were looking for don't forget to take photos and write down all of the information you find on the head stone.

Sometimes the inscription will be worn and hard to read. One way to help with this issue is to take at least 2 photos of the stone. One needs to be a close up photo of the headstone one so you can clearly see the inscription area and one at a bit of a distance away.

A close up photo with the right photo computer program you may just be able to enhance the photo enough to make out what the head stone says.

The Census Records are valuable resource for a genealogist. They can give you a lot of information and confirm where an ancestor lived. It can give a person's birth year and where they were born.

When dealing with the census records though keep in mind that they have evolved and changed over time. Some are quite basic in what information was recorded and others are more detailed.

You can access the **1790** through **1940** census records as of now. The **1950** census should be available in 2022.

The first United States Federal Census was done in 1790 as the Heads of House Holds. This census covered only very basic information and did not list everyone in the house, just the person who was considered head of the house.

The information that the censuses collected over the years had changed adding more information or changing the way it was asked. The census records that can be found today date every 10 years from 1790 to 1940.

Now you need to know that the 1890 census records were involved in a fire in 1921. The fire caused a lot of damage to it and many records were lost. A few bits and pieces of it did survive that may be of use to you though they can be hard to find.

If the records you want have been destroyed for that year there are several special schedules that had been done that year that may be of some help to you.

The census records can be found usually at some libraries, Historical Societies, National Archives. There are several good internet sites for researching Census records. Of Course Ancestry is one as is Family Search.org but 2 little known web sites are www.censuslinks.com and www.census-online.com.

They both are free to use and have census records other countries besides the United States as well. They also have made them easy to use.

While you are doing your research there are many pitfalls you can avoid that will lead you right into a brick wall. If you know what they are you can try to avoid some of them.

You will run to a brick wall at some point in your researching, we all do. But there are things that you can look out for that will help you to avoid them.

There are more common things you can watch out for (Mistakes that can be made) that will help you in avoiding brick walls.

Not getting and using family group sheets can lead to problems that can be time consuming. These group sheets are an important research tool that will help you to keep track of the information you already have and what you need to look for. They will be the foundation of your research plan.

Being organized is a necessity in genealogy that can be over looked at first. Well organized records will keep you from repeating research you have already completed or losing documents and information.

Keep a copy of your information at home during your research trips. Information can be lost or miss placed. You need to make sure you have a backup copy in case something happens to your working copy.

Making photo copies of documents and records you find is important and often can be neglected. Thinking that because you write it down some where the information you find on them is good enough can be a mistake. It is one that will send you in search of it again.

Not keeping track of where you find your information and creating a cite list can be a mistake that is often made. A cite listing for every document and information you find will save you time and trouble if you need to go back to the source for more information or to confirm for others where you got the information from.

Some beginning researchers may **not think of looking at the histories** of the area their ancestors lived in. In the histories you may be able to find an ancestors biography, information on your ancestor as it relates the history in that area.

You need to know though that **some of these "histories" may contain mistakes** or information that someone other than the actual ancestor told to the author of the book. You need to verify information that you find or are given to insure its accuracy.

If not you could be led down the wrong path and run into a brick wall causing you to retrace your steps. This includes other family histories a relative or someone else has done as well. Always be excited over the information but be cautious and verify the information any way. It could save you some time.

You will need to find out the time table for the formation of the county and townships in the area where your ancestor lived. These will determine where to look for documents and information on your ancestor.

Your ancestor could have lived in Springfield Township but the year he started living there was before 1805. If you were to search for him you may find him listed as living in Wolf Creek Township for a few of his records and it's not because he moved it's because the boundaries did.

If the difference in the boundaries occurs with Counties as it did with the townships then you would need to search both counties for his records and information. Records did not move to a new county even though the boundaries changed they stayed with the county they were first created in.

Hand writing and its interoperation has led to some names being forever changed or documents not being recognized by genealogists as the ones they are looking for.

   a. Old hand writing styles can cause confusion for not just transcribers but for us as well. The styles of hand writing have changed over many generations and have come from many other countries. This can make it hard to read by its self but it can also make it harder to read if the person doing the writing was not a very neat writer or did so in a hurry. There are many tips and tricks to help out with this problem the best one I can tell you is to use the internet or books on old hand writing.

b. Accents of our ancestors and those who took names for records. Accents of our ancestors and those who took names for records. The accents of our ancestors and those who wrote down the information and names have sometimes created mistakes. Depending on whether or not the information taker was able to understand the pronunciations correctly of a name. Or if they did not ask how a name was to be spelled and just assumed it was spelled as it sounded this could change the actual spelling of the name you are looking for. For example Colter could be spelt as Coulter or Lean spelled as Lain. It is not unheard of for a family member was the one giving information and got it wrong themselves as well.

Middle names did not become a common practice until about the mid to late 1800's until that time they were rarely used. By the time the 1900's came to be it was almost standard practice for a child to have a middle name. Middle names have caused a lot of confusion for many genealogists over the years whether or not they knew the middle name to begin with. Many people have used only their middle names in their lives even on important papers and documents and then some have used their middle names on some documents and yet not others. Knowing the middle name of your ancestor if they had one can be important to know for this reason.

Nick names can also provide their own brand of brick walls for you to overcome. A nick name typically is a shortened version of their full name such as Cathy is for Catherine but then there are a select few who have a nick name that is not related to their full name. Someone

I know has a nick name that is this way. He goes by the name of Pat but his real full name is Melvin. No one would ever put Pat with Melvin. His wife had a similar nick name situation. So try to be mindful of them as well.

Don't believing every detail in a family story that has been handed down through the generations in your family. As in the children's game Telephone, the story is likely to have changed by the time it reaches you. That's not saying that it is all wrong. You just need to make sure you verify the details before accepting them as fact. They do hold many clues and information on your family but you need to verify the information and make sure it is accurate.

Be aware that there are non-family members out there that have the same name and birth dates that are very close to your family members. That can lead you astray if you do not verify that you found the right person. They even may live in the same location as your ancestors

For example you find that there are two John Smiths living in Mercer County both born with in one or two years of each other? How do you know which one is your relative? You use what you know already. The census records depending on the year will show family members and their ages. You then compare the two John Smith's census records and find out who the family members are and their ages. Then compare them to those family members who are attached to your John Smith to find the one that is yours.

All in all the best thing you can do while researching is to Verify all of the facts and information that you find with what you already know and with official documents and records. It's why you start off with what you know.

There are vast amounts of websites available for genealogical research. The key is to know how to find them and what you are looking for. You can find anything from message boards, blogs, to County Histories and scans of documents and records online.

Google search bar and Google books is an excellent place to start a basic search if you know what you are looking for. Just by typing in the google search bar the information you are looking for you can access a wide variety of information that may lead you to other web sites that can help you.

For example when I put in James Luther Griffin I get images of him and his grave site, is page on find a grave as well as long with many other sites that have nothing to do with the man I am looking for but it is always worth doing.

I have found plenty of wonderful surprises I had not expected to find this way. The Google books site is wonderful for when you are looking for a book that may have your ancestor in it or for a county history. The catch is though you will find many books you can actually read cover to cover that will be of some help to you but there will be books that are listed that you cannot access.

The upside to this is it may give you a lead on where you can find the book such as Amazon or a chance to find it in a library. The web site will give you the information you need to find it easily. If the Library does not have the book you need they may be able to get it through the interlibrary loan program.

There are Genealogy web sites such as Ancestry.com that for a fee will give you access to their vast data bases. There are also many web sites such as Family search.org that are free to use.

Family search will give you summaries of documents and records and maybe even scans of these documents or links to access them. They will link even to ancestory.com some of the records though you may not be able to see the original document.

I find if I cannot find what I am looking for on Ancestry.com I will turn to Family search and sometimes get links back to Ancestry with what I was looking for in the first place.

US Gen Web is another one that is organizes other genealogical web sites by state and county. There is a World Gen Web Project web site as well. Roots web.com is another free genealogical web site that also has data bases mailing lists and message boards that can be a great tool to use along with its World Connect Project of family trees.

Find a grave is a great web site to use when looking for a grave site and obituary. It is a free website with the option of searching for a person's name or cemetery name or even search it by location.

Interment is another free web site for cemetery research.

National Archives is a fee based site that you can order records from if you know enough information about the subject of your search. It may be able to provide you with military records census records and more.

Even the County Court Houses tend to have web sites that may contain data bases that may be of use to you such as Historical Land Records available online. They should contain information on their hours of operation and the various offices they have. They may also give you information on the types of records they hold and the time period for them. Sometimes they will help you locate the information over the phone or through the mail. Keep in mind though if you visit the Court House yourself you have more of a chance to find additional family members that maybe you had not thought to look for there. Some Court houses have indexes for their Birth, Marriage, and Death records. That comes in handy when researching.

Other important places for research there are many Historical and Genealogical Societies, Libraries. Each of these places will have a wide variety of information and books for researching. Some of the things you may find here are census records, local histories, state histories, family genealogies, military records and newspapers on microfilm or as clippings. They usually have websites and can be contacted over the phone, mail or you can visit. Keep in mind some even have local history books for sale that you may not be able to find elsewhere so ask if they have any. You just may be surprised how much information you may find on your family in these kinds of books.

*May the brick walls you find be small
and the way over them easy.*

Notes: